MIRACLES OF PSYCHIC PHENOMENA

Other books by this Author:

Experiences of Trance, Physical Mediumship and Associated Phenomena with the Stewart Alexander Circle: Parts One, Two & Three.

Touching the Next Horizon: Experiences of Trance and Physical Mediumship with the Stewart Alexander Circle.

What is the Next Horizon? A Study of Unusual Happenings on the Path of Your Life.

MIRACLES OF PSYCHIC PHENOMENA

by

Katie Halliwell

© Katie Halliwell 2025

All rights reserved. No portion of this book may be reproduced or utilised in any form or by any means, electronic or mechanical, including photocopying, recording or retrieval system, without the prior permission in writing of the publisher. Nor is it to be otherwise circulated in any form or binding or cover other than that in which it is published.

First edition 2025

Published by
Saturday Night Press Publications
England

snppbooks@gmail.com
www.snppbooks.com

ISBN 978-1-908421-68-5

www.snppbooks.com

Dedicated to

Janette, Christopher and Adrian:

They passed away in 2024
and afterwards
chatted to me in my dreams.

Also to
Ann, Judy and Michael
who passed away in 2025.

My appreciation goes to:

Tom and Ann Harrison and their
'Saturday Night Press Publications'
for its much valued information on Physical
Mediumship and Psychic Phenomena,

to Ann Harrison for her assistance in verifying
and editing this book,

to various authors helping to spread the truth
as they know it to be,

to my readers for sharing their own personal
experiences of Psychic Phenomena,

to Christine and Claire for their continuous
support in my research.

CONTENTS

	INTRODUCTION	9
1.	The Lady on the Train	13
2.	The Miracles of Psychic Phenomena	17
3.	Thought	24
4.	The Tarot	30
5.	Marjory	36
6.	Reaching Out	41
7.	Life Goes On	49
	CONCLUSION	57
	Appendix 1	61
	Appendix 2	67
	Book List	73

Introduction

My previous book *'What is the Next Horizon? – A study of Unusual Happenings on the Path of Your Life'* was to bring about an awareness of extraordinary senses.

Since its publication, I have had interesting feedback from readers telling me about their own experiences and asking further questions.

Quite often, such personal stories are kept under wraps for fear of being ridiculed because they are to do with some form of psychic and/or physical phenomena the logical brain fails to understand.

So – what is it that moves us beyond our five ordinary senses?

Well – a very well known Master did come to enlighten us ... but do we, to this day, fully understand how the miracles were performed?

As such experiences have been around since the dawn of time, it is my long held belief that the miracles of Jesus were based on psychic phenomena and my findings are explained here in the first two chapters and in the Conclusion.

In my opinion, these miracles really did take place and it has been said that my suggestion makes a lot more sense – to such a degree that it can bring us closer to Him with a far greater understanding.

Why limit ourselves to faith when there is knowledge?

There is a lot more to the life of Jesus than meets the eye.

Of course, it is up to you to decide for yourselves what happened over 2000 years ago and if this booklet is not suited to your beliefs, then you might like to shelve it until such a time it becomes more palatable.

Personally, I do not belong to any man-made religion and class myself as a free spirit according to the natural law. A law which brings about the way we look after ourselves and others, the way we think and the way we focus on the greatest service of all – love.

Isn't that exactly what Jesus came to teach?

A sense of belonging is important to us all and this is where 'love' comes in, and it all depends on how we think.

Thought is a powerful process ... it creates.

It creates a way of life and it is how we make it which brings together a greater sense of reality.

But do we really understand our thoughts?

Are we answering our own questions or do we seek advice from others?

Do we really know where our path of life is leading us?

Is this the reason why Tarot and Angel cards appear to be popular?

And when it comes to people having awesome experiences of actually seeing and physically touching a loved one in spirit – a very surreal encounter – who do we tell and who do we turn to when something like this happens?

Have you been subjected to anything similar?

What you are about to read might help bring all of the above into perspective.

Maybe in reading these accounts you'll discover that you are not alone.

Chapter One

The Lady on the Train

Whilst sitting on the window seat travelling on the train to York, a stranger – a very nice lady – came and sat next to me. She started chatting telling me she was going to meet somebody in York, do this, that and the other and I told her that I was going to visit the Treasurer's House, (a National Trust Property) have lunch then go to the Spiritualist Centre.

Suddenly the lady went very quiet and warned me not to go to the Spiritualist Centre. She announced that she was a born-again Christian and as she got a little book out of her bag, she asked me if I followed Jesus.

This is how the conversation went:

(K – Katie / L - The Lady).

K   *Follow Jesus?....Of course; we do what he did over 2000 years ago.*

L   *You haven't read the bible.*

K   *Yes I have. I have studied every line and page of the bible from start to finish and it did not answer my questions. I've visited various Christian Churches and they couldn't answer my questions either.*

L   *What sort of questions?*

K   *Well, for one, where is heaven?*

The lady did not answer that question and quickly opened her little book asking me to look at a verse which said "Follow me for I am the light". I looked at it and said, "*Yes we do follow Him by healing people and giving out love, but of course not to the standard of Jesus because he is a very high soul ... and the spirit people do materialise just as he did.*"

 L *Oh, you can't do what Jesus does – he is 'The Son of God'.*

 K *Ah – well, it seems obviously clear that we are not on the same wave length here, so it might be an idea to stop the conversation at this point.*

But the lady did not stop.

 L *Jesus can save you, you need to be saved from the darkness of the medium.*

and she carried on ...

 L *When you see this medium, think about the lady on the train and Jesus will save you.*

In my late teens, I had studied the bible in fine detail and did not find any answers to my questions, but during my later years, I was to discover Spiritualism and started to study psychic phenomena. With this new found knowledge, I began to see Jesus in a different light and in fact, various clergies of the Church, (two outstanding names being Rev. G Maurice Elliott and the Rev. G. Vale Owen) had also come to the conclusion that the miracles performed by Jesus were actually psychic phenomena.

Going back to my experience with the lady on the train, she was so determined and insistent, in such a dominant way, that I should listen to her she wouldn't let me leave my seat. I eventually got really upset and wanted to move away particularly after her remark of me 'being saved' from the darkness of a medium – yes, there are fraudulent mediums, but no way should she talk about true genuine mediums like that.

Because I was sitting by the window and somewhat hemmed in, I had to stand up and ask her to let me go, but she wouldn't budge and everyone in the carriage was looking at us – it was so embarrassing.

Eventually, she did allow me to move.

Feeling quite disturbed by this experience, I was relieved to be able to sit in another carriage, but wondered why I had allowed the lady to penetrate my aura. I felt offended and I became somewhat angry. I sent a thought out to my spirit friend Freda Johnson[1] asking why I could not control myself and why did I get myself into such an emotional state. I sat there thinking, I am not as strong as I thought and with all the knowledge I have, I failed to keep calm for the sake of spirit.

The train arrived at York and I quickly moved off the platform to avoid bumping into the lady.

As planned, I visited the Treasurer's House, had lunch and arrived at the Spiritualist Centre, quietly tip-toeing in because Stewart Alexander[2] (who was to demonstrate his physical mediumship later in the afternoon) was in the middle of giving a talk about human weaknesses. He was explaining how even the best mediums had their weaknesses, and as he talked, I could not believe what I was hearing – it was if that talk was made for me after what had happened and ... I felt so much better afterwards.

Was this a case of synchronicity[3]?

---

1. Freda Johnson is one of Stewart Alexander's spirit guides.
2. Stewart Alexander is a renowned physical medium of our day.
3. Synchronicity is a series of coincidences occurring in a person's life suggesting a connection or message from the Spirit World.

Facts, Theories and Anomalies relating to this Chapter

Subject – The way we think.

It is a well known fact that most people could not read and write in the biblical and medieval days and back then, they had no choice but to follow (and in some cases) be misled by another man's thoughts. Hence the famous phrase 'The blind leading the blind'.

Nowadays we can truly think and investigate for ourselves.

In Spiritualism, there are no pearly gates or eternal punishment, but there is retribution for one's actions on the earth plane.

Heaven is not a place but a state of consciousness and every spirit will find itself at a comfortable level according to its own development. There are many levels of planes/spheres in the Spirit World with the Astral World being nearest to Earth, this probably explains that famous phrase – 'In my Father's house are many mansions'. Thought is the creative force behind these planes/spheres as you will be reading about in Chapter Three.

More and more people found comfort in Spiritualism especially during and after the two world wars and in my opinion, with the knowledge I now have, I feel so much closer to Jesus, with a far better understanding of what could have happened in those biblical days.

Although some people like to see Jesus as the 'Son of God' and others like to see Him as a prophet, to me he is a highly evolved living soul guiding us along the path of love and light and I believe that those miracles performed over 2000 years ago were actually psychic phenomena.

In the next chapter, I will cover aspects of this in more detail.

Chapter Two

The Miracles of Psychic Phenomena

Psychic phenomena are experiences that go beyond our ordinary senses and are often attributed to spiritual forces.

The bible is full of these wonders and they are still happening today.

Because people without knowledge of psychic phenomena may have no conception of what could have happened over 2000 years ago, this makes me wonder if the sacred book was translated and copied in its true colours.

I do not think it was.

As nobody had access to the original script, we will never know what really happened in those biblical days and considering all this; maybe I should express my own thoughts on Jesus.

With our knowledge of psychic – and in some cases physical phenomena – let us take a look at what could have happened when those miracles were performed.

Jesus walked on water. (*Molecules can be changed.*)

Spirit does have the ability to change the molecules of their mediums enabling them to dematerialise and re-materialise in another place, just as Alec Harris did, when he literally disappeared from the chair he was securely bound to, in a locked séance room, and ended up on the landing outside. On another occasion he re-materialised in the front garden and rang the door bell to be let in.[1]

Stewart Alexander's wrists were firmly fastened to the chair arms by locked cable ties and yet, in a demonstration of 'Living Matter through Matter' Stewart's arm was freed when it went right through the cable tie itself, leaving the cable tie around the solid arm of the chair.[2]

If D. D. Home[3] could float out of a window and hover in mid air above the streets – then I wonder if he used the same technique as Jesus did when he walked on water.

A Voice is heard at Jesus' baptism. (*Could be independent direct voice.*)

In the account of Jesus being baptised in the river Jordan it is said that a voice was heard coming from the air in the form of a dove[4] saying, 'This is my beloved son in whom I am well pleased.'

This is known as independent direct voice and is frequently heard in good circles. By direct or independent voice, a spirit person can speak to a group of sitters; the voice can be heard from mid air by means of a voice box made of ectoplasm extracted from the medium.

---

1. Alec Harris (1897-1974) was one of the world's most brilliant materialisation mediums in the mid 1900s.
2. You can read about this in my book *'Touching the Next Horizon'*.
3. Daniel Dunglas Home (1833-1886) was a great physical medium with an outstanding ability to levitate.
4. There have been occasions where spirit doves and birds have been known to fly around the séance room.

An example of this was told to me by my friend Georgina Brake: a group of people were chatting in a well lit room when they heard her deceased mother's voice speaking from the direction of the ceiling after the medium went into trance.

This also happened in Stewart Alexander's Circle. One night the sitter to the left of the medium became aware of a voice down beside her knee. The voice continued speaking quite clearly for several minutes before asking Tom Harrison[5] to pass on a message to a mutual friend, requesting that the friend visit the circle so that they could speak together. This was achieved a few months later.[6]

One of the most well known direct voice mediums of modern times was Leslie Flint, whom you will be reading about in the next chapter.

Feeding the 5000 with five loaves and two fishes. (*Possibly apports or manipulation of matter.*)

Apports are objects that appear out of nowhere, such as coins, badges, flowers which are transported from one place to another and this doesn't only happen in séance rooms. Tom Harrison told of his physical medium mother's surprise when she opened a walk-in pantry door to find it was absolutely full of gorgeous sprays of lilac complete with its wonderful aroma, an apported gift from spirit on her birthday– March 17th[7]. She had been in the pantry moments before but had

---

5. Tom Harrison (1918-2010) was the son of an excellent physical medium Minnie Harrison (1895-1958).
6. *'Experiences of Physical Phenomena in 21st Century'* by Ann E Harrison (Chapter 17).
7. Lilac doesn't blocm in March in the North-east of England. The full story is in Tom's book *'Life After Death - Living Proof'*.

forgotten the sugar for their tea and opened the door again.

Another biblical instance of this is:

Turning water into wine. (*could be by apporting it or changing of the molecules.*)

Those who have eyes to see – let them see. Those who have ears to hear – let them hear.

What more can I say other than this is now known as Clairvoyance, – the ability to see spirit, images etc. and Clairaudience, – the ability to hear spirit.

There are a number of personal examples of this in Chapter Four, when my medium friend gave me a sitting, and also in Chapter Six.

Jesus spoke with Moses and Elias. (*Physical contact with spirit.*)

When Peter, James and John went up with Jesus into the mountain where it would be dark with perfect conditions for a materialisation séance, they saw Moses, Elias and Jesus talking together. Just as we now talk to our deceased loved ones in a physical séance with the use of a substance called ectoplasm.

Ectoplasm is energy taken from the medium through any of the orifices and develops from the invisible to the visible to clothe the spirit person. Once fully developed, the materialised spirit can then move around talking to the sitters of the circle and will be solid and warm to the touch.

If the medium is sufficiently developed, and there is enough energy, the spirit form may be seen in red light as recorded in Louie Harris' and Tom Harrison's books.

There was one special occurrence in an Alec Harris séance. A policeman who had worked in India had a conversation in Hindi with a spirit who had known him there, and that same evening a Belgian sitter conversed in five different languages with a materialised form who had been a victim of a Concentration Camp.

Spiritual Healing.

There are many accounts of Jesus doing healing recorded in the four Gospels, and of the disciples continuing it in the later chapters of the Bible. Many small and great acts of this are still happening today. Notable healers of modern times are Harry Edwards in the mid 20th Century, George Chapman in the late 20th Century, and Matthew Manning today.

Speaking in many tongues. (*speaking in a language previously unknown to them.*)

When an external consciousness (spirit) takes control of the medium in trance, they can and do speak in their own native language as happened at Pentecost in 'Acts of the Apostles' Chapter Two, when the disciples were touched by the 'Holy Spirit'. It is recorded that 'devout Jews' from different regions and countries were able to hear what was said in their own languages. The disciples were Galileans so unlikely to speak any other language.

This ability is known as Xenoglossy (a term first used by Prof Charles Richet in 1905). It is often associated with trance mediumship, while some think of it as a manifestation of a higher intelligence or spirit control.

In Maxine Meilleur's book '*Great Moments of Modern Mediumship - Volume 1*' there is a section on this phenomenon, including details of some of the mediums through whom this occurred. One in particular was Carlos Mirabelli who is said to have to have spoken and written in more than thirty languages.

These are just a few of my suggestions for the phenomena and we must not forget of course one of the prime:

Jesus rose from the dead. *(In ectoplasmic form.)*

In the Gospel of St John there is an account of Jesus materialising in front of Mary Magdalene, three days after he had been crucified. Mary didn't initially recognise him. When Red Cloud, the guide of medium Estelle Roberts[8], was asked why this was, this is what he said:

> "Mary took Jesus to be the gardener. Now then, Mary must have known the gardener to have mistaken him for Jesus, ... but the gardener was asleep in the garden and the Nazarene took the ectoplasm from the gardener, clothed himself in it because Mary was not clairvoyant. Therefore in the moulding of the atom it was the gardener's influence which Mary detected."

When Jesus said to Mary "Touch me not for I am not yet ascended to my Father," it could be that Jesus told her not to touch him knowing that the ectoplasm would shoot straight back into the medium (the gardener) causing serious damage to his health.

---

8. Estelle Roberts (1889 – 1970) was a renowned clairvoyant and trance medium. This quotation is from *'The Medium Discourse : Red Cloud's Inner Teachings'*, compiled by Brandon J. Kim.

Another point to mention is that Jesus would have been able to choose his disciples spiritually by being able to see their *auras*. The aura is the energy field surrounding the body, and is made up of emotional, mental, and spiritual emanations of that person. By these He would have known their powers and mediumship abilities.

When Jesus said to his disciples, "Greater things than this shall ye do when I go unto the Father," he was meaning that psychic phenomena would continue on indefinitely.

You can read about hundreds of cases in the books '*Great Moments of Modern Mediumship - Volumes 1 and 2*' compiled by Maxine Meilleur.

It is most important for me say that, in my opinion, Jesus did not come to teach religion and as stated in the conclusion of my previous book '*What is the Next Horizon?*' – He came to teach love.

* * *

Facts, Theories and Anomalies relating to this Chapter

Subject – Psychic and Physical Phenomena.

You have, of course, the freewill to Google any of this information should you wish to, or as an alternative, you could read my other book, '*Touching the Next Horizon*' . This offers unique details of many of the physical phenomena that happen in the Stewart Alexander Circle.

For a Clergyman's view on the phenomena of the New Testament see Appendix 1.

Chapter Three

Thought

In 1937, the Archbishop of Canterbury, Cosmo Gordon Lang, set up a committee of twelve prominent individuals under the chairmanship of Dean Francis Underhill[1,] to investigate the claims of Spiritualism. Several prominent mediums sat for them.

It is understood that two thirds of the committee were in favour of recognising Spiritualism as true and that communication with the 'so called' dead was indeed possible.

However, much to the dismay of Francis Underhill, Lang refused to publish the report[2].

To Archbishop Cosmo Lang's way of thinking there was a good reason for not publishing the committee's report. Apparently he considered it dangerous for people with extremely material minds to sit in a séance and rightly so, because the only protection from lower entities is true spirituality.

His main concern was – how spiritual is Spiritualism?

This is also an important question we need to ask ourselves.

---

1. Francis Underhill was the Dean of Rochester before becoming the Bishop of Bath and Wells in 1937.

2. Nine years later a copy of the report found its way to the desk of the Editor of Psychic News. After carefully verifying its authenticity it was published in full in the paper, and later as a pamphlet.

The loss of a loved one can be devastating and this is when most people seek a spiritualist medium. Many do so with expectations and are extremely disappointed when they don't get a message.

This happened to me. As explained in my other book, *'What is the Next Horizon?'* I expected my mother to come through various mediums and she didn't until I realised how self-centred my own thoughts had been.

Meeting Robert and Georgina Brake, (two very spiritual mentors) put me on the right path and they emphasised that one should never sit in a séance without an experienced medium. Researchers craving for proof (as I did in my early days) and those with curious thoughts, who choose to dabble in their own inexperienced ways, are delving into the unknown without knowledge of protection – which brings me to understanding Cosmo Lang's concern.

Cosmo Lang died on 5th December 1945.

In May 1959 Lang, in spirit, returned one evening to speak through the well-known direct voice medium, Leslie Flint. Direct Voice (also known as Independent Voice) as explained in the previous chapter, is where a spirit person is able to speak in his own voice via a voice box made of ectoplasm emanating from the medium's body.

In this communication he expressed the danger of attracting earthbound souls of low order who are only too anxious to distort the message through many an inexperienced medium or seeker.

Like minded spirits are attracted to one's own thoughts and because of this; we need to be careful of how we think. It is imperative that we stay clear of 'wanting' and negative thoughts especially when sitting for spirit communication.

Having loving thoughts with a genuine desire to help others is the key to a successful séance and a sincere opening request for protection is always advised.

Focusing healing and uplifting thoughts towards others does help to build up the right kind of atmosphere and by doing this we automatically attract the protection of caring and loving spirits of a higher source.

They see the radiance in our auras. Hence the phrase: – follow me for I am the light – in other words, think as Jesus would. This to me has more meaning because a strong bright aura full of light enhances healthy conditions.

Love creates radiance.

Love is the binding force of our heaven on Earth and as stated in the previous chapter, heaven is not a place – it is a state of condition.

This can be confusing because so many of us have been taught that heaven is a far away distant place, when it is not.

The spirit people actually occupy the same space but in a different dimension/vibration.

To help explain what I am trying to say… picture this:

You are wearing a headset and are playing the game of paint ball using virtual reality.

The game becomes so intense that you lose yourself in the woods whilst targeting your opponent.

You are, at that time, occupying the same space but in a different – illusionary– dimension created by the computer.

While you are so deep in the woods and hunting around the trees, you are not aware of the actual room where the game has been set up and will be completely oblivious to it until the headset has been removed.

The same thing applies to the physical body. It is a natural computer providing the five senses you will need to live your life on this Earth.

Like the trees in the computer game, everything on Earth will look and feel very real until death releases us from our physical bodies and you will then find yourself in the Spirit World – your heaven which occupies the same space but in a different dimension.

On this great school called Earth, we are responsible for our actions and as we learn how to develop our way of thinking, we can do two things:

a) Choose to follow another man's thought by not thinking for ourselves or

b) Ask our own questions and try answering them.

Have you ever tried doing this?

When we start to answer our own questions, we then begin to wonder where the answers are coming from.

Do the answers come from us or from Spirit?

*　*　*

Facts, Theories and Anomalies relating to this Chapter
Subject – Thought and Direct voice.

Where does inspiration come from and why should we doubt ourselves when we are spirit in a material body?

In fact – What is thought and where does it come from?

Here is an excerpt from my other books, *'What is the Next Horizon?'* and *'Touching the Next Horizon'*:

"If you sit back and really think about this, it might help you to know that thought has no language. For example, if you wanted to pick up a piece of paper, do you actually think in WORDS, I ... am ... going ...to ... pick ... up ...the ... paper? Or – do you just do it?

You just do it of course; it is the natural motive of your consciousness, the same consciousness that lives on after so-called-death.

Everything in the Spirit World is instant with no need for language, therefore not only do the spirit people have to slow down to our vibrations, they also have to use the spoken word to communicate with us, a procedure which is not a necessity in their world.

The Spirit World communicates through the power of thought. So when you suddenly, for no reason at all, think of a deceased loved one, it is likely that the consciousness of that soul has blended in with your aura attracted by your love, and that is how, in some ways, your loved ones in spirit can get closer to you now than they could when they were on the earth plane.

Always remember that they are only a thought away and like-attracts-like plays a big role in the acceptance of unconditional love."

As far as I am concerned, I see the brain as a physical instrument that dies at physical death and 'thought' is the living soul that survives – the real you.

Stewart Alexander, (our physical medium) attended a Leslie Flint séance and his spirit guide White Feather (a North American Indian) came through and spoke to him in Direct Voice. It had been noticed that whenever White Feather over shadowed the medium in trance, Stewart's left hand would immediately begin to curl in upon itself as if grossly deformed. Visiting Leslie Flint was an opportunity for Stewart to ask White Feather direct if during his earthly life he had had a physical deformity. Instantly he replied, "Do you mean my left hand?"

Leslie Flint was a virtual stranger to Stewart and knew nothing of his guide or any of Stewart's personal mediumistic development. Those six words "Do you mean my left hand?" confirmed to Stewart that White Feather was indeed his genuine guide, a true spirit who once lived upon this Earth. You can read more about this in Stewart's book, 'An Extraordinary Journey – The Memoirs of a Physical Medium'.

The 'Leslie Flint Trust' offers over 80 recordings (including Lang's communications) not only of famous people who came back to talk to the sitters, but people from all walks of life. To listen to any of the recordings and to find out more about this well known medium – visit – www.leslieflint.com.

When the Rev. Pearce-Higgins announced on TV in 1960 that he had a recording of Cosmo Lang speaking from the "Dead" it sparked the interest of *The Daily Sketch* who carried out an investigation and issued their findings in a pamphlet *"Life After Death"*. (See Appendix 2).

As a matter of interest Agnes Abbott – Tom Harrison's Aunt Agg – was one of the mediums who gave a demonstration to the 1937 Committee. She was renowned for her platform mediumship before her passing in 1942 and she had sat with Arthur Findlay in 1936. He added an account of this sitting in his famous classic, *'On the Edge of the Etheric'* a book providing compelling evidence for both the researcher and sceptic. From 1946 onwards she materialised many times at Minnie Harrison's Home Circle. Photographs of materialisations of Agnes can be seen in Tom Harrison's book *'Life After Death – Living Proof'* [3]

---

3. Also on his DVD *'Visitors from the "Other Side"* available from Saturday Night Press Publications, (not available for USA), or on the internet at: https://www.youtube.com/watch?v=4Xyk8tXfPTQ

Chapter Four

The Tarot

Having discussed our thoughts and how we think, whether materially or spiritually, the same thing can apply to tarot readings.

A materialistic approach to a tarot reading is often looked upon as fortune telling whilst a spiritual tarot reading is totally different and can be an uplifting experience.

Here is a prime example of a spiritual reading I had on the 15th March 2015. I did not request this reading; a medium friend of mine had a sudden urge to get the tarot cards out and as she laid them out, amazing evidence came through from spirit.

Even though the medium is a friend, she had never met any of the spirit people who communicated and most certainly did not know anything about the precise personal details expressed through the tarot card reading.

I would like to invite you to contemplate the reading as it was conveyed to me. My thoughts and conclusions during and after the reading are shown in italics.

* * * * *

My friend, using the cards as prompts, started the reading by telling me that she was linking with a man with receding hair. She went on to explain (in a symbolic way as she looked at the cards) that he was putting on his suit and tying up his shoelaces with the intention of getting ready to go somewhere, albeit very cautiously, she said it was my Dad yearning to come through, but he was not comfortable with venturing to the earth plane because he was somewhat frightened of not being able to return to the Spirit World.

When he was on the earth plane he suffered some sort of bilious attack.

True: Dad was often sick and suffered a lot of indigestion.

He always needed to finish something he was doing, did not like leaving anything undone.

True: He often stayed outside in the street tinkering under his car in all weathers to get the job done, (even under torch light).

He wanted to say sorry for laughing at your spirit work.

True: He did laugh at and ridicule my spiritual work.

My friend then went on to mention that two ladies were supporting him; the one on her left was someone wearing an apron indicating a character who had to work; an ordinary person who would often hang back.

On her right was a lady she could only describe as a Barbara Cartland type, someone who loved finery, shoes and smartness.

Correct: My Mum would always hang back at public gatherings and was never confident enough to meet anyone above her status – (although she would be the life and soul of any party once she got going). Myra (my stepmum) was just the opposite, she was very forward and outgoing and although she was not like Barbara Cartland in character, she was very refined in her attire and loved shoes. The two ladies I believe were my Mum and Stepmum.

My friend then described a triangle – Dad was at the front of the triangle towards me and the two ladies were at the back at both sides of the medium. She went on to tell me that these two ladies were working closely together urging Dad to move forward – he needed help and had much to understand.

Dad (via the medium, as she read the cards) confirmed that he was very happy in the Spirit World which suited his own lifestyle, but he had not got much confidence in making contact through any mediumistic communication especially by the use of tarot.

He also informed her that he was shocked to see my Mum when he passed to spirit in 1991, (my Mum died in 1976 and she must have come for him).

I would consider this as being correct as Dad, having no knowledge of life after physical death, would have been shocked to see my Mum, especially after he had told me before he died that he did not want to leave Myra (my Stepmum), who was at that time still alive on the earth plane.

The two ladies were encouraging Dad to move forward and would remain together until he progressed. They had seen my light which was helping them to develop a greater understanding of the spiritual work I am involved with.

It is nice to know that my Mum and Stepmum have accepted one another and that they are working together.

I was advised not to be chained down too much on my work.

Dad (through the medium) then announced that he would have to go and lie down because he couldn't handle the communication any more.

This makes sense because on Earth, Dad would often lie down on the settee when he was tired or when he felt a bit sick.

The medium then mentioned that bluebell woods were being brought forward.

Back in the dim and distant past (before bluebells became a protected species) it was an annual ritual for our family (along with others) to pick these lovely flowers.

Robert and Georgina Brake, good friends of mine, (known as Bob and Ena) then came through and encouraged me to set up a special room in my house as they had a special spirit room in their home – a church within.

True: They did have a special room in which they would spend much time meditating and sitting to connect with spirit. Bluebells have a strong connection with Bob and Ena – it was the bluebell wood nearby that led to their decision to buy the house they were to move into at Bradley near Huddersfield back in 1988.

The medium then explained to me that the link with bluebells was one set of informants going off and another source coming in.

Dad and Mum use to take me picking bluebells back in the 1950s and 60s – so they would be the informants going off and Bob and Ena would be the other source coming in.

Bob and Ena told the medium that I would be writing another book after the one I was writing.

(At that time I was writing a book about my life from birth up to 1999 which is now in print titled 'What is the Next Horizon?')

They brought lilies and the medium suddenly became absolutely overwhelmed by this contact – a feeling of a higher force; they were white elongated lilies.

Correct: The white elongated lilies were Bob and Ena's favourite flower and they are also the symbolic flower of the White Brotherhood.[1]

Overcome by this mass of white lilies in front of her, she started to lose her voice as she spoke. In fact there was so much energy coming from these lilies she announced frantically that she could not see my face as a powerful mist of energy was building up in front of her.

The medium then had to bring the reading to a close because the energy was too intense for her to continue.

* * *

Facts, Theories and Anomalies relating to this Chapter

Subject – Tarot Reading.

To be honest, I was never really interested in tarot readings until my friend introduced me to it.

I have to admit that the communication was brilliant and it was very interesting to hear how my Mum and Myra (my Stepmum) were getting on together in the Spirit World because when Myra was alive on the earth plane, she was very concerned about how she could love my Dad and be with him in the Spirit World when my Mum would be there.

I am sure many of you will have asked a similar question.

---

1. The White Brotherhood is a group of highly evolved souls who have the welfare of those on earth at heart, expressing absolute pure love.

As food for thought, marriage on the earth plane plays an important and necessary role to the law of the country; whilst at the same time; unconditional love is the true essence of the Spirit World. It doesn't matter how many deceased husbands or wives you have in heaven, because love overpowers individuality and we are as one united whole. (Although I understand soul mates do remain together.)

And there is another point I would like to mention. When Ena was alive on the earth plane, she would often tell me that I was the daughter she never had, expressing a feeling of motherly love. Ironically, all three of them, Mum, Myra and Ena came through the tarot reading which happened to be on Mothering Sunday, (15th March 2015).

Coincidence or not? Who knows?

Although I have never used Angel Cards, they are like Oracle cards and appear to be extremely popular for those who wish to try out their own version of Tarot.[2] However, as one interprets the chosen picture *(which is governed as to how one thinks)*, we do need to be aware that self-centred thoughts will create negative impressions.

True sincere thought, particularly with the urge to help others, can have the ability to make spirit connections in its own specific way, but what about physical happenings of contact outside the field of thought?

When spirit does make such a breakthrough, we certainly know about it as you will be reading about in the following chapters.

---

2. Oracle and tarot cards are both used for diviration and guidance, but they differ in structure and interpretation. Tarot cards follow a set structure of 78 cards with established meanings, while oracle cards are more flexible, with no set number or structure, allowing for greater intuitive interpretation and diverse themes.

Angel cards are a type of oracle card deck that focuses on providing uplifting and positive messages of guidance and support from the angelic realm. Unlike Tarot cards, angel cards generally do not contain negative or challenging messages.

Chapter Five

Marjory

Some people have had spontaneous experiences of physically feeling spirit in solid form and seeing their deceased loved ones.

There are even those who have had out of body experiences along with those who find themselves astral travelling.

I would like to start this chapter with this true account from a friend.

Marjory and her husband Rob had been together since they were teenage sweethearts and were devoted to each other, so much so, that I would consider them to be soul mates. Rob died of a brain tumour in 2004 and Marjory was absolutely devastated. After Rob's passing, Marjory started to ask me questions and I did my best to comfort her by exchanging letters in the hope of helping her to cope with her grief. In one letter dated 1st January 2005, she had something extraordinary to tell me.

> "I have some strange and wonderful news for you, but I'm having a job to take it all in myself at the moment. It's all so strange and over whelming, without you to talk to, I'm sure I would begin to wonder about myself. I need help to understand what is happening.
>
> I have been in bed for 2 days, really unwell with some kind of flu bug. I woke early yesterday – it

was still dark. I made myself a glass of milk, put a CD in the machine in my bedroom and went back to bed with my drink.

I fell asleep; the next thing I remember was the CD coming to an end. There was a soft warm glow, like soft sunshine coming through a curtain, but it was a dull day and I was looking at the blank wall. I turned over to Rob's side of the bed and he was there, beside me, just lying there on his back smiling. I moved over and put my head on his shoulder, I could feel him, feel his skin, his breath. I ran my hands across his shoulders and felt the strange little bones that protruded from his muscles. I felt his hands and the little stubby finger which had been chopped off at the knuckle in an accident; I kissed it and held his hand. I ran my fingers through the soft hair on his chest. I turned away to his photograph to thank him for coming to me, and when I turned back, he was still there beside me. We didn't talk, we didn't need to. It was so wonderful.... I am crying now, but not with sadness. I was at peace in his arms. I just closed my eyes and stayed there until it all passed over me, which seemed a long time.

I was so calm, happy and relaxed; I can't explain the feeling of inner warmth.

The bereavement meetings come to an end on 10th January, but I couldn't have told them all of this. It's all too close and personal, they might not understand. You are the only one I can talk to Katie; I do hope you don't mind. Just tell me if things are too heavy for you, I will understand."

This was such a detailed description of her wonderful connection with Rob, her deceased husband who appeared absolutely real and solid to the touch. Many people would doubt the validity of such an experience, dismissing it as a vivid dream, as Marjory's family did.

But Marjory knew it was real, she knew it was not a dream and she didn't understand it.

I often wondered how this could have happened.

Marjory was on her bed relaxing to the music and when she closed her eyes – did she unknowingly go into a heightened state of consciousness enabling her to reach the Astral Plane?

Apparently not every spirit form witnessed is deceased. In this same letter, Marjory told me about her mother's experience. It was not a deceased loved one her mother saw, but her husband living on this earth far away in another country.

> "I remember my dear Mum telling me that during the war my dad went missing in Africa. In the middle of the night she woke up and he was standing beside her bed in full uniform with his rifle in his hand. He waved to her; she called out his name, and then he was gone. She said she knew straight away that he was safe because he never ever came home with his rifle. Days later she received a message to say he was safe in a military hospital with diphtheria. My Dad was the last man on earth to believe in anything I am telling you, but something happened."

Did Marjory's Dad astral travel?

Who knows?

I believe it is possible that he did.

* * *

Facts, Theories and Anomalies relating to this Chapter

Subject – Physical connections and out of body experiences.

Marjory's experience was very precious indeed but of course, she will never be able to prove it. It was Rob's own special way of making that connection with her.

After reading my book, 'What is the Next Horizon?' a friend of mine, Sheila told me how she felt her deceased mother beside her in bed. Here is her true story:

> "Whilst not a believer like you, even the sceptic in me feels there is more to us than our earthly bodies. I have, in fact, had a couple of experiences myself, the first being when I lost my Mum (who was my best friend) whilst my husband was involved in fracas in the Middle East – very traumatic time! I was dreaming my Mum was cuddling me to comfort me and as I woke, I physically felt her rise from the bed.
>
> Being a Yoga lover like you, I relish the relaxation period. I only once achieved what I deemed to be total relaxation when "I" was looking down on me lying on my mat – a truly surreal experience."

And here is another true account:

Louie Harris also had connections with her beloved husband in spirit whilst lying in bed – here is an excerpt from her book about her deceased husband Alec Harris.

> "Twenty four hours later, at about the same time as he had passed over the night before, Alec returned to me.
>
> As I lay on my bed, I felt a man's hand, strong, warm, and well materialised, take hold of my arm and gently squeeze it in the old familiar loving way. My heart was eased. Soon the blessed sleep, which had evaded me, took me into soothing unconsciousness.

> *A few weeks later I had a remarkable experience. Again I was lying on my bed. I was on the point of entering the sleep state when I felt the weight of a body as someone lay beside me. I felt no fear, only a sense of keen expectancy. An arm reached over my waist; it was warm, strong and solid. A hand took hold of mine across my body, as it had so often done in the past. I knew beyond doubt that my Alec had come back.*
>
> *Then I experienced a strange sensation. In a flash I found myself out of my physical body in an astral projection. I saw Alec standing in the room. His whole being seemed to be bathed in a mystic blue light. He appeared so much younger than when I had last seen him, no more than 30. I went to Alec. He placed his arms around me, murmuring tenderly, 'I had to come, Lou ... I had to come.'*
>
> *I remember putting my arms around his neck, gazing up at his thick golden hair, the waves highlighted by the soft Spiritual light. 'Oh, Alec,' I said. 'Isn't it wonderful to be together again?' Suddenly, I felt a strange trembling sensation. With a jerk that left me breathless I was back in my physical body."*

It would appear that drifting off into the sleep state tends to be a perfect opening for spirit to draw close particularly when the brain is less active.

Have you had any such similar experiences?

I personally find this interesting because when I am drifting off to sleep (or meditating) I sometimes see spontaneous clear pictures in colour; black and white or sometimes in a negative type image. They always appear in a flash – long enough for me to be able to register before opening my eyes and wondering why I should I see a man on a bike or a scene of a white house in the country.

Could this be the Clairvoyance in me?

Chapter Six

Reaching Out

As well as seeing flash images, spiritual dreams also appear to be my forte. I know they are spiritual because they are so real, clear, in colour, sometimes precognitive and I even have conversations in these dreams. They also leave me with strong feelings when I wake up.

These lucid dreams are entirely different to ordinary dreams created by an over-active brain.

Allow me to tell you about a very close friend of mine.

Janette and I were there for each another, without being in each other's pockets. We loved to go on long walks, often foraging for mushrooms, watercress, and berries; in fact, the bilberry picking in summer became a yearly ritual we would look forward to. We knew each other so well that we would enjoy our banters to the point of bouncing off one another.

Janette died on 31st January 2024.

Janette has one brother, Andy, who lives in the Highlands of Scotland – they too were extremely close, so much so, they would telephone each other almost every night.

Andy and I were both devastated when we were told that Janette had only weeks to live – it was pancreatic cancer that took her physical life.

All three of us believe in life after death, and Janette bravely accepted her illness with grace even when she was in so much pain. She sold her car, got herself organised and told us she did not want a funeral.

She wanted us to remember her as she was and to celebrate her life in our own special ways.

Like me, she is a free spirit and not tied to any man-made religion.

Although I am unable to prove the evidence of Janette communicating with us, I can tell you what happened.

We all have our own different ways of tapping into the Spirit World however slight it might be, and on Friday 9th February 2024, my sister Christine thought of setting up a joke on one of our friends. As soon as she mentioned her idea, she suddenly sensed Janette on her right saying, "Yes – go for it – do it."

The impact of this sensation shook Christine so much that she put her hand to her chest and said, "Oh – Janette – oooh – she just nudged me."

But of course Christine could not prove what she experienced and felt it strange that Janette should come to her and not me, but I understood why. It would be because my aura was darkened with grief and that can block out any possible spirit communication.

On Wednesday 13th March I had a lucid dream of Janette walking with me on my left-hand side, her energy was very strong and it was quite surreal and uplifting as we conversed with one another. She showed me her right index finger. It had a nasty scratch across the bottom half of it.

I said, "I have got some plasters," and started to look for some – there were big trays in front of me full of food and as I moved them, there was a tray of games with a draughts game box on top. I moved that and then found a tray of plasters – but they were not the right size. I then looked in my bag and found some more plasters and pulled out one. Janette said, "That will do," and took it.

When I looked at the pavement we were walking on, I got the feeling we were in the Blackpool area and I started telling Janette about a séance where Gilbert[1] (her cockatiel) was flying around – nothing wrong with his wing.

I said to Janette (who was still on my left hand side) "I still can't get my head around the fact that you are going to die within the next few months – it seems awfully strange."

I woke up with a strong feeling, thinking – yes – it is strange that Janette is going to die in the next few months – then I suddenly realised where I was and thought – no – hang on – she has already died.

The dream was so real it took me some time to realise where I was when I woke up. This dream left me in awe, but wondering what was happening.

When I told Andy about the dream, he would not accept it because he thought Janette should have gone to him first – and rightly so. He also told me that it was too early because people who die of an illness sleep in the Spirit World for about two years.

But – here is a question – can he prove the two-year sleep?

I naturally felt upset for Andy.

This was his belief and mindset as he wished it to be.

---

1. Gilbert was Janette's pet cockatiel. He had a damaged wing, he also loved eating chips. My medium friend had told me, back in 2022, she clairvoyantly saw Gilbert flying around her séance room and then eating a chip held in his claw.

So I stepped back.

Later on, on Monday 25th March 2024, I got a text from him.

This is what he said:

> "I don't know if it is significant, but as I dozed off last night, I had a vision of me in the bottom of a well, looking up to a small circle of light and someone (not recognised) looking down and trying to say something, but incomprehensible."

As soon as I read the text, I instinctively knew the person at the top of the well would be Janette, but I did not have the heart to tell Andy because I knew he was grieving too deeply – so my reply was:

> "I am just wondering if someone is trying to reach you, but because you are so deep in grief, the connection cannot be made. The good thing about this is that someone is there trying to help you and may try some other method later on."

Andy accepted my suggestion.

I had a second dream on Tuesday 4th June 2024 and it was just as lucid as the first dream. It started with me in my car driving to Janette's place and ahead of me the road was fully blocked by a resurfacing machine. I saw a car drive onto the pavement on the right and I did the same. I also remember seeing pebbles being swept away by a road worker with a brush to clear a drain. This was followed by another road on the way to Janette's place which was beautifully cobbled. (In reality that same road has a tarmac surface.)

Then suddenly, I was conversing with Janette (again she was on my left side) and as we walked around the area where she used to live, I saw some beautiful buildings – a row of old large houses in Cotswold's style. I marvelled at this beautiful scene and remarked that I never knew these buildings were here. Janette told me that they had been there all the time. The next scene was a bicycle upside down in a kind of carport – it was a mountain bike and was obviously being maintained. I said to Janette, "Isn't that bike too big for you; you are not going to manage it." Janette replied, "Of course I will – no problem – everything will be fine."

I woke up.

Again, it was quite surreal and I knew these beautiful buildings would be the type of houses Janette would love and the bike – well – although she could never ride a bike when alive on the earth plane, the dream meaning of a bike is working towards fulfilling one's destiny.

As these two dreams were so lucid, had I been able to tap into the Spirit World allowing us to meet, and was Janette showing me those houses in her heaven which occupies the same space but in a different dimension?

I am certain that this is what happened.

Two days later, on Thursday 6th June 2024, the medium friend in the Blackpool area sent me an email to tell me that when she was coming out of séance the other evening, she went ice cold and clairvoyantly saw Janette with Gilbert, her pet cockatiel, on her right shoulder.

Janette told her that she was happy and had visited her old home and she would help Claire (my niece) to get a home – then went as quickly as she had appeared. The medium thought it was odd Janette mentioning Claire and not me or her brother wondering if by helping Claire she was maybe in some way thanking me.

Very soon after, Claire announced that her partner had at long last managed to sell his business and that they could now start looking for a house (a new home) in the north of England.

Coincidence or not – I will leave that to your own conclusion.

Between 9th February and 6th September 2024, there were nine different types of signs altogether (along with possible spirit communications) concerning Janette with myself and various other people, but rather than put these in, I would now like to discuss the above sources of spirit connection.

* * *

Facts, Theories and Anomalies relating to this Chapter

Subject – Spirit Connections.

Andy rejected my first dream because Janette should have come to him first and I do perfectly understand him. But isn't it strange that he should have the vision of the well.

Did Andy's idea of the two year sleep create a blockage?

After all, the spirit people cannot interfere with our freewill to create our own thought forms, so, maybe we should all keep an open mind, who knows, Janette could have been trying to make that breakthrough and it would be upsetting for her if we dismissed any hints – however small – of her efforts to reach out to us.

Here is a sign of a different kind:

Out of the blue, a friend gave me a donation for our charity, the 'Hearing Dogs for Deaf People' in memory of Janette.

The fund-raising manager's reply to my friend was an email letter dated 17th May 2024 and it included a heart-warming story about a hearing dog. This is what she wrote:

> "This special gift will help our work to change the lives of deaf people like Laura and her hearing dog Meg. Laura lost her hearing gradually during her younger years and was then profoundly deaf by her early 20's. She found this a very difficult transition and became severely anxious, emotional and isolated, and tried to conceal her deafness from the outside world. Since meeting Meg, Laura says "Meg is just like my shadow. She is a part of me, and I don't know what I would do without her. She has completely changed my life and given me the greatest gift, the ability to feel safe, protected and able to achieve my dreams."

It hit me like a ton of bricks – I could see words in this story strongly related to Janette and me, (a phenomenon known as Synchronicity). So, did Janette's aura blend with the fund-raising manager's thoughts helping her to choose this particular story as, more to the point, – Janette used to take a friend's dog out twice a day, rain or shine, and she fell in love with this dog – so much so she did not want to leave her behind.

The dog's name was Meg.

Stop press

While this chapter was being edited, I received an email from Andy (who is a mechanic) on Saturday 24th May 2025.

> "I had a very strange event at work with a colleague as witness. My phone was in my top left hand chest pocket as I was discussing a job. It started ringing and

I got it out, but as my hands were covered in oil and grease, I asked Ben to open it up and see who was ringing and to answer it while I found a rag to wipe my hands on, which he did. I heard him say "Hello" 2 or 3 times before he passed the phone back. When I looked at the screen, the caller was Janette. I have her phone, but have not charged it in over 12 months. When I got home that evening, I dug the phone out and sure enough the battery is flat, so HOW?"

Somehow or other, Janette is doing her best to make that breakthrough and incidentally, my niece Claire got the keys to her new home on Tuesday 29th April 2025.

Chapter Seven

Life Goes On

Janette had the right kind of thoughts to be able to recognise some extraordinary experiences, however minor or insignificant. She wrote them down for me... the next four pieces are in Janette's own words.

1. Smells and Extraordinary Experiences

I can honestly say I have never 'seen' anything that could be described as other worldly, but I often experienced strange smells that suddenly fill a room, even when the doors and windows are closed. There was one instance though...

In 2002, about three weeks before my husband passed away – a traumatic time before the life machine finally had to be switched off – I was in the house by myself and saw the light in the hallway slowly rotating, it turned one way and then back again with the panels of the light shade making patterns on the wall. There was no explanation for it. The bedroom windows were open and there was no breeze whatsoever during this still summer night in June.

At the same time, what really caught my attention was an unmistakable smell of fish and chips, just as if someone had walked in with them, (there were no fish and chip shops anywhere near the house) the smell filled the hall and halfway up the staircase.

About ten minutes later, my stepson came home and he too could smell the fish and chips. The smell lingered for some time and then cleared, just as suddenly as it had manifested.

My Nanna (now in spirit) use to work in a fish and chip shop during the war years and she often told me of the smell lingering on her clothes and in her hair.

Was this phenomenon of smell, her way of letting me know that she was with me? Knowing what grief I was about to face in three week's time.

I like to think so.

In July 2002, my husband sadly passed away.

Later that year, I decided to have a new bathroom suite fitted and had to carefully consider what I could afford and because the cost was preying on my mind, I kept asking myself, "Should I, – shouldn't I?"

My husband had died, and I was on my own with no-one to bounce ideas off; then one morning while still considering my options, I found the small shelf on the bathroom wall hanging precariously by one screw. Having no idea what had caused the shelf and rawlplug to come away from the wall, I took it as a message from my husband to get on with a new bathroom.

The work was completed in three weeks and as soon as possible, being proud of my achievements, I enjoyed the luxury of my newly installed shower before going downstairs to relax in the lounge. I had only been sitting for five minutes when there was an overwhelming aroma of cigar smoke. My husband used to enjoy a good cigar and once again, I like to think that it was him creating this manifestation to let me know he was happy with the bathroom.

Since then, I have often experienced the same strong cigar smoke along with other smells like flowers, perfume or something baking in the oven.

I do have an extremely strong sense of smell and wonder if this type of phenomena might be my own special way of identifying a spirit connection?

Although I do dream of places – and in colour, I very rarely see anybody or speak and most of my dreams are forgotten after waking up.

However, back in 2001, I did have a dream that was significant. I was looking at a child's school exercise book. It had a blue cover and contained lined paper. There was no name on the book and no entries had been made, except on one page, six numbers were written at the top with each number separated by vertical lines, they were 2 | 9 | 10 | 13 | 16 | 22.

The dream continued and in it, I was on holiday with my husband in a hotel in Filey (a seaside town on the East Yorkshire coast). I had bought a lottery ticket and knew I had won £10. My husband insisted that I go down to the reception desk and make certain. The receptionist checked out the numbers and said, "Yeah, you've won." I then went back upstairs to tell my husband that I had definitely won £10.

Since having that dream, I used those same numbers, sometimes I won £10, but more often nothing at all.

In September 2002, I was on holiday in Filey with my parents and brother – the first time without my husband – and whilst I was there, I bought a lottery ticket and was delighted to find that I had four numbers when the draw took place.

When I returned home, I went to the post office with my winning ticket and was surprised when the cashier asked for some form of identification which I didn't think was necessary for four numbers, but the cashier told me I had five numbers and had won £982.00.

So – was the dream I had in 2001 a precognitive indication of winning such an amount to help pay for the bathroom in 2002? Was the phenomena of the revolving light and the fish and chip smell my Nanna letting me know that she was with me three weeks before my husband died? Was the phenomena of overwhelming cigar smoke my deceased husband expressing his satisfaction of the new bathroom?

I like to think so.

2. Astral Travelling

My Dad, suffered a stroke and between 2002 to his death in 2010, he continued to have a series of mini strokes or T.I.As. He was also diagnosed with Alzheimer's which thankfully never progressed to its full potential.

We moved him into the small bedroom to ensure Mum could get the rest she deserved.

It was in that period that he would often describe waking up during the night to find another man in bed beside him, (bearing in mind, he was in a single bed) and would ask the man who he was, but the chap never answered and my Dad would often climb over him to get out of bed.

This situation went on for months and my brother Andy who lives in Scotland told me of his extraordinary experience:

> "I woke up sometime during the night and as I opened my eyes, Dad was there, standing beside my bed. I heard him say:

"Go back to sleep lad. I was just checking to see if you are alright."

Andy wasn't curious as to why Dad was there, how he had got there, or why, and it wasn't a dream. He was definitely awake at the time but then turned over and went straight back to sleep.

This experience was so imprinted in Andy's mind that to this very day he vividly remembers clearly seeing his Dad in the darkness of the bedroom.

When Andy was told about Dad describing a man laid on the bed beside him, we both wondered if this was a case of Astral flight.

3. Imaginary Playmate

Our Dad, was born in November 1928, the youngest of four children.

His older brother and sister had been born at least ten years earlier with only a two year age gap between them, but there was another sister born in 1922 but sadly died of infantile fits before Dad's arrival into this world.

He told me on more than one occasion how he would play in the garden with a little girl who would just turn up out of the blue.

He would be outside playing for such a long time, so much so, that Grandma would often have to call him in for his meals. When my Dad described his little playmate to his parents, his father would be reduced to tears because he had unknowingly described his deceased sister perfectly – even down to how she wore her hair and the colour of her dress.

As he was only four years old, my grandma would always keep an eye on him when he played out and had never seen anyone else in the garden; to all intents and purposes he had been entirely on his own in the garden.

I would also like to mention that my Dad had not seen any photographs of his deceased sister.

4. Clairsentience

My brother Andy has always had a sense of something that was going to happen, a kind of premonition. For example when he was once driving on a straight road in the Trough of Bowland, he suddenly felt a strong need to slow down, causing his passengers to ask why he'd taken his foot off the accelerator. Suddenly from behind a wall of trees a tractor came right out in front of him. Had he been going at normal speed, he would have crashed into the tractor.

He is also sensitive to certain areas, especially where something emotional had happened in the past.

One day as he was walking over a field on a hill, he sensed a feeling of depression with his hair standing on end – we were to later find out that this was known as Hanging Hill.

In another area he sensed a feeling of foreboding, and again we were to later find out that on this spot there had been an uprising with many a poor soul slaughtered.

Whenever he visits people, he can always sense the atmosphere in their home whether it be good or bad.

* * *

Facts, Theories and Anomalies relating to this Chapter

Subject – Clairesentience.

When you walk into somebody's house, do you pick up a sense of feeling about the place?

If so, then you could have the gift of Clairesentience.

Most people have this sensation to a greater or lesser degree and as it is such a sensitive gift, we need to protect ourselves from negative energy.

This is part of what the aura is for, an egg-shaped bubble, to protect us from unseen damaging forces and as the aura can change colour according to our instinctive feelings, this natural intuition can tell us to stay away from such detrimental sources.

We now live in a troubled and invasive world of technology advancing with a frightening speed, so much so that it makes it more difficult to relax and meditate. Although we are in such a world, we must always remember that we do not have to be of it.

The brighter the aura, the better and to create a healthy aura, we do need to make time to relax, meditate and spend more time in natural surroundings like the countryside or in the garden. Not only is this a self-healing source, it is also a good connection to the Spirit World, a chance to develop an ability to recognise the occasional psychic phenomenon, however small, should it occur. It could be the opening to one's own personal discovery of spiritual enlightenment.

Clairesentience is a wonderful gift, firstly of being able to walk into a place and sense feelings. When the feeling is good and uplifting, then that energy is an awareness of the occupants having the right kind of thoughts similar to your own... an introduction to the people you need to be with. On the other hand it is a useful tool for mediums to feel the presence, personality and emotions of spirit people around them during a sitting for someone.

Mixing with people of like mind will help maintain mediumistic faculties and if you are at a loss as to where to find that kind of source, perhaps the list of suggestions below might help.

* * *

The Saturday Night Press Publications is a good site to visit on the internet; in here you are likely to find a book to suit your type of mediumship and spiritual needs or for information on good mediums of the past and their work. (www.snppbooks.com).

You might like to visit **Stewart Alexander's website** on https://stewartalexandermedium.com particularly if you are interested in Trance and Physical Mediumship.

Spiritualist National Union (SNU) is a religious organisation that supports spiritual healers, spirit mediums, public speakers and teachers as well as supporting Spiritualist Churches all across the United Kingdom. They also have development courses at Stansted Hall known as the Arthur Findlay College.

For those who wish to remain as Christians but are interested in Spiritualism, any **Christian Spiritualist Church** could be more suitable to your needs or **The Churches' Fellowship for Psychical and Spiritual studies.**

If Meditation, Philosophy and Spiritual Unfoldment is your choice, then **'The White Eagle Lodge'** is the site to visit.

All of the above can be found on the internet.

Conclusion

So – was Jesus a medium?

I would say a definite YES – and – He is a very Spiritually Evolved soul.

After all, he did say "Greater things than this shall ye do when I go unto the Father" meaning that the disciples would be able to continue using the psychic phenomena – and it is still happening now.

Did the later copyists and translators of the Bible understand what he was saying?

I think not.

A really good book, 'Mediumship: Our Heritage' by Kate Maesen explains all. For example, here are two excerpts detailing how easily the Bible had been misrepresented:

> 1) "In any study or discussion of the Bible many variables must be taken into consideration, for instance, the language of the day was limited; certain translators have not agreed on all the vocabulary. When Jesus was on earth his native language was Aramaic, although he knew some Hebrew from his studies in the Temple. It is logical to realise that no book could go through as many translators as has the Bible without being coloured by the personality of the translators. Another point to be considered is the fact that except in rare cases, the people were uneducated and could not

understand, as even our elementary school pupils do today."

2) "It is an actual fact that no other book on earth has undergone so many changes and alterations at the hands of the copyists, the old scribes, as has the Bible, both the Old and New Testaments. Even the well versed Bible scholar cannot say for certain which, are the words, sentences or chapters that have been intentionally or accidentally left out, overlooked, misread, and misinterpreted by the copyist. Furthermore, not one of the scribes who made the copies that we have today, including the new translation, had access to the original text but only to copies of the still earlier copies."

Another excellent book I would highly recommend is *'Red Cloud's Inner Teachings'* by Brandon J. Kim, which I quoted from in Chapter Two. This 'Medium Discourse' (two volumes combined into one) authentically produces the original material from Estelle Robert's séances held in the 1930s.

Estelle's spirit guide Red Cloud talks about the Nazarene, i.e. Jesus, in fine detail and more to the point, what we should truthfully know about him.

It is our entitlement to tap into the Spirit World; after all, we are spirit in material bodies and it only takes one good psychic phenomena experience to change our way of life ... once acknowledged, never forgotten.

However, I appreciate that many will not have had such an opportunity, but there is nothing to stop you believing. If you prefer to follow another person's thoughts then by all means do so, but be careful of fixed mindsets which can trap you into a rut. It is healthier to keep an open mind, and by doing this, it will enable you to think for yourself.

Thinking for ourselves and using our freewill to find our own understanding of truth – as we know it to be– may not always be correct especially at our level of limited knowledge. This is when experiences step in to be our teacher

As you will have read in Chapter Five, Marjory could not understand what was happening to her, and Sheila – even though a sceptic – she had had her own surreal occurrences. These personal experiences were so strong, they could not be ignored by the recipients, and as we might spontaneously encounter such happenings ourselves, whatever they may be, we should always acknowledge them with respect.

There are different ways to experience psychic phenomena.

My forte at the moment appears to be in the form of dreams and I hope that Chapter Six has helped to emphasise how my friend Janette has been trying hard to make a spirit connection breakthrough to Andy.

She finally succeeded with the 'telephone call'.

Do you feel there is more to us than our earthly bodies?

If so, why not venture out and discover people of like mind. We are all in the same boat, as pupils living on this great school called Earth, so it might be worth sharing our untold happenings.

It was Janette's wish to share her own and her family's unusual happenings as you will have read in Chapter Seven.

Such happenings are often spontaneous and they come when we least expect them. They cannot be induced, but tend to come about when we are either in a relaxed frame of mind – perhaps in meditation or when we are going through an emotional time – but when they do occur, do we know enough about what is happening?

If you have not already done so, it might help to read about my own personal experiences in my book *'What is the Next Horizon?* This book could point the way to a few more answers and once you start to seek in a positive way, then you might have a better understanding of a way of life as you choose to it to be.

Will it be your Heaven on Earth?

It is possible to make it happen and I wish you every success in finding it.

* * *

Appendix 1

The Churches' Fellowship for Psychical and Spiritual Studies is a Christian organisation founded in 1953 to explore and integrate psychical and spiritual experiences within a Christian context. It aims to study and investigate paranormal and relevant phenomena, including psychic science, and their significance for the Christian faith. The Fellowship also provides support and guidance to those who have experienced spiritual gifts, bereavement, or a desire for deeper spiritual understanding.[1]

In the 1960s Dr. Mervyn Stockwood, Bishop of Southwark, had this to say about the work of the Churches' Fellowship for Psychical Study[2].

"I have no patience with people who just write the whole thing off as humbug and fraud.

"I think the work the Fellowship are doing is important because it is a subject that demands careful and thoughtful enquiry.

"Our job is to examine the evidence without pre-supposition or jumping to conclusions.

"The weakness of the Church has been its refusal to consider the evidence or discuss it."

In collaboration with the Fellowship the journalist Neville Randall held an investigation for the 'Daily Sketch' into reports they had received.

1. https://www.churchesfellowship.co.uk
2. The original name for the Churches' Fellowship.

The following is one section of the pamphlet – *'Life After Death'* – that they published[3]. Printed here as it was published (in the 1960s).

NO LONGER BY FAITH ALONE

The evidence produced by psychic research into life after death is of vital interest to Christians everywhere.

For this evidence is throwing new light on the Bible and bringing some of its messages up-to-date.

In some strange way the information which purports to come from the next world ties up with the evidence of the Gospels.

It makes it easier to understand them.

And it is making it possible for some who found it hard to believe in the Resurrection of Jesus by faith alone to believe now through reason.

This has happened to many people. But the story I am going to tell you now is what happened to an ordained minister who still had reservations.

He is the Rev. Bertram E. Woods, 60-year-old Minister of Horley Methodist Church, Surrey. He recently became the honorary secretary of the Churches' Fellowship for Psychical Study.

Here is his story in his own words:

Rev. Bertram Woods

---

3. This pamphlet is not to be confused with the book of the same name by Neville Randell mentioned in the Book List p74.

"Although I was an ordained minister I never really believed completely in the supernatural element in the gospel story.

Above all, in the story of the Transfiguration as told to Matthew and Luke. Or the fact of the Resurrection and the appearances Jesus made to his disciples after it.

"These major problems were always in my mind:

"How could Moses and Elias, who had been dead for hundreds of years, have been seen talking to Jesus in the presence of Peter, James and John, as Matthew and Luke report in the story of the Transfiguration?

"How could Jesus after His crucifixion appear to His disciples suddenly in a room which was bolted and barred? And then disappear in the same way as He appeared suddenly and without passing through the door?

"My reason made me say these stories were not true. What-ever the explanation it was not as the writers of the gospels reported.

"Then I was introduced to the study of psychical matters by my wife. I investigated cases, including a number of mediums and the phenomena they claimed to produce.

"I became convinced that these psychic phenomena are genuine. There is no doubt that people can receive impressions from others through something other than the five physical senses.

"There is another force, not subject to the laws of the physical universe, which can produce physical phenomena like moving objects without human agency.

"As I accepted the reality of these phenomena, the problem of accepting the supernatural events in the New Testament disappeared.

"I now have what is to me a perfectly satisfactory explanation for everything that happened.

"The whole concept of a life beyond death has become clearer. The things that happened to Jesus after His crucifixion have been revealed by psychic phenomena to be normal events within the experience of ordinary human beings after death. Take the story of Jesus appearing to His disciples on the Emmaus road after He was crucified. This is similar to experiences which people now living have had.

"These have been witnessed and corroborated in recent times.

"Some are common knowledge.

"Like the case of Shackleton and his two companions during a particularly difficult trek near the South Pole.

"Instead of two companions he saw three. When they compared experiences all three said they had seen the fourth figure.

"I have come across many corroborated cases such as people walking along roads becoming aware of a companion who disappeared suddenly – just like Christ.

"These psychical phenomena do not *explain* the Resurrection and other supernatural events in the Bible.

"But they prove that these things are in the range of human experience.

"I do not believe that the things Jesus did were unique marvels never seen before or since. I think that as well as being the divine Son of God, He was a truly human being.

"The kind of body that Jesus had after death is what St. Paul meant when he spoke of the spiritual body which we shall all have.

"**Modern psychic investigations confirm that St. Paul was right.**

"The old idea of the physical body rising again after a long sleep seemed impossible. It probably is impossible. You don't have to believe it.

"My investigations have convinced me that the supernatural stories in the New Testament can be taken as they are written. They don't have to be explained away. For many people today the mere proclamation of the gospel story is not enough. It is not as convincing as it used to be. They want proof.

"Now at last modern scientific research may offer the proof that they are looking for. The proof that Christianity is true and real."

The experience of this Methodist minister can probably be paralleled in clergymen all over Britain.

At least one Church of England parson believes that the interpretation of the Bible through modern psychic discoveries can revitalise faith in Christianity.

He is the Rev. John Pearce-Higgins, Vicar of Putney.

"What is so baffling to modern man," says Rev. Pearce-Higgins, "is the knowledge of scientific facts which make bodily survival so improbable.

"High explosive destroys bodies utterly. So does the sea. So almost does cremation. It is hard for anyone to believe that a few ounces of dust scattered in a Garden of Remembrance and soon blown to the four quarters of the earth can ever be reintegrated to form a physical body.

"**Therefore they are puzzled and fall back on blind faith, or deny the fact of survival, claiming that the death of the body is the end of consciousness and life.**"

This, says Rev. Pearce-Higgins, is due to centuries of false teaching about the resurrection of the physical body.

If we read Paul correctly, he believes, he tells us that we already have our spiritual body.

And that when we die, the husk of the material body falls away or is discarded, and that the true and eternal spiritual body survives.

This brings us back to where we started. For the accounts of death from Gordon Burdick[4] – as told in the Grace Rosher story, and from other people who claim to have survived it – describes an almost exactly similar process.

If you believe them, you must believe the New Testament, too.

AND IF YOU BELIEVE THE NEW TESTAMENT ALREADY, THE EVIDENCE OF PSYCHIC PHENOMENA CAN DO NOTHING BUT SUSTAIN YOUR FAITH.

* * *

---

4. This is referencing a previous section in the same pamphlet which says:

Gordon Burdick, a life-long friend of Grace Rosher wrote through her pen in Automatic Writing) ("Beyond the Horizon" 1961).

"... he described his first sensations after his death. He said he was met by his mother and others of his family who had died before him. He thought he must be dreaming.

Then he told her about his new life. He had another body now, he explained, an etheric, or spiritual, body which was interwoven with the physical body during life on earth but released at death. It was like the physical body, but without deformity or blemish.

"You don't feel any different except that you haven't any pain or feeling of weakness.

"There is no greater truth than that there is no death. There is no such thing."

Appendix 2

This is a second article from the 'Daily Sketch" pamphlet.

A VOICE FROM THE DEAD

CAN the spirits of men and women who have died REALLY communicate with the living?

For thousands of years this question, linked with speculation about life after death, has intrigued men's minds.

In September, 1960, ten million viewers saw and heard a Church of England parson declare on Television that he had a tape recording of a message from Cosmo Lang who was Archbishop of Canterbury at the time of the Abdication and who died in 1945.

The parson was the Vicar of Putney, the Rev. John Pearce-Higgins.

He was speaking in ATV's Sunday evening programme 'About Religion' which was discussing the relationship between Christianity and Spiritualism.

Rev. J. Pearce-Higgins

If the spirits of men and women who have died can really communicate with us, does this proof of survival after physical death sustain our belief in the teachings of Jesus and the Christian Church?

It is a question the Church dodged consistently until the Churches' Fellowship for Psychical Study decided it could be ignored no longer.

If the message from Cosmo Lang is genuine, the question is now answered.

When Dr. Lang was Archbishop of Canterbury, he set up a committee of experts under the then Bishop of Bath and Wells, Dr. Francis Underhill, to examine the evidence of psychic phenomena.

After two years they reported that "certain outstanding psychic experiences of individuals make a strong prima facie case for survival and for the possibility of spirit communications."

They added: "We think that it is probable that the hypothesis that they proceed in some cases from discarnate spirits is the true one."

And they recommended that representatives of the Church should keep in touch with developments.

Cosmo Lang never allowed this report to be published. It is still officially secret today.

Dr. Cosmo Lang

If the message from Cosmo Lang is genuine, he now realises that this decision was wrong.

We have heard this tape recording. And we have heard the voice which claims to speak for Cosmo Lang say:

"Where Spiritualism was concerned I was afraid of it. I was afraid it could undermine the Church and probably even destroy it, and I was not sure that it had very much to offer that was good.

"Of course many of these ideas I have now changed. I do feel very strongly that it is a thing that is so vital and so important that all peoples should be conscious and know about it.

"But I do feel that it is dangerous if it is used in the wrong sense."

Later on he explains what these dangers are.

"If you are to contact the highest forces, the good forces, those who can help the world, those who can uplift mankind, you must have instruments (mediums or sensitives) who are of like mind and of like thought, and, as I said, it seems to me that many of these instruments are of a very, unfortunately, low order."

The voice goes on: "While you are, as it were, only scratching the surface of the Astral worlds which 90 per cent. of your instruments seem to be doing, then it is not only bad, but it can even be dangerous, because like can attract like, and also lower entities who are earthbound, who cling to your earth can come through and use your instruments, and also through instruments speak to peoples, and tell peoples of things which are not true, and also be the cause of much unhappiness, much misery."

Is this the voice of Archbishop Cosmo Gordon Lang speaking to us from the next world to solve our problems?

If not, who is it and where does it come from?
The known facts are few and simple.

The words we have quoted are part of a longer message which took 20 minutes to deliver.

It was recorded by Mr. Sidney Woods, a 66-year-old retired farmer who lives in Brighton and is a brother-in-law of the Bishop of Bury St. Edmunds.

On a morning in May, 1959, he was sitting in a room in Westbourne-terrace, London, W., with a colleague, Mrs. Betty Greene, and an elderly medium through whom he had obtained tape recordings often in the past.

Without warning the silence was broken. A voice, speaking slowly and with difficulty, said "Hello, hello – Cosmo Lang here."

It came from a point about four feet above the ground and three feet to one side of the medium's head.

The message followed. Slowly at first, then with more confidence. It continued for 20 minutes and ended just after the tape ran out.

The medium has been investigated thoroughly and his honesty and integrity have never been in question.

The opinions are not so straightforward. In an effort to test its authenticity, the tape has been played to dozens of people who knew or heard Lang.

They were nearly all churchmen or churchgoers. Nearly all of them said they thought it was Lang. But none of them could be 100 per cent. sure.

Lang died 15 years ago. The memory of a voice unheard for 15 years loses its clarity.

Here are two typical opinions.

FIRST The Rev. John Pearce-Higgins, Vicar of Putney and Chairman of the Central Research Committee of the Churches Fellowship for Psychical Study.

"Provided the seance was genuine I think the probability is that it is Cosmo Lang."

It bears all the signs of Lang. Those who have heard this tape and Lang say that the voice is very similar. It's just the sort of thing he would say.

"When you take it in conjunction with a lot of other similar types of communications which can be more accurately corroborated, it seems probably true."

Second opinion comes from the Hon. Mrs. Herbert Lane, daughter of the late Lord Rockley. She lives near Wareham, in Dorset.

Lang was a family friend. He used to stay with them frequently. She stayed with him when he was Archbishop of York.

She told us: "My first impression was that it is genuine. As far as I could see it felt like him talking. I feel it's exactly what Archbishop Lang would say. It was just like him not to criticise – without putting forward constructive ideas."

Can you go further? As this message is so crucial, the 'Daily Sketch' staged a test which we hoped would be decisive.

From the Director of Religious Broadcasts at the BBC we borrowed a record of the living voice of Cosmo Lang. It was the famous broadcast he gave on the Abdication of King Edward VIII in 1936.

We took this and the tape recording said to come from Lang to the home of the Bishop of Southwark,

Dr. Mervyn Stockwood, and played them one after the other and then both at the same time.

The Bishop had with him his Chaplain and the Principal of St. Stephen's Theological College, Oxford.

The test was not decisive. The voice of the living Lang was stronger and firmer than the voice from the dead. But that could have been because in the nine years between the Abdication and his death he grew old and his voice grew weaker.

"I assume," said the Bishop "we can rule out any possibility of conscious fraud. Where the voice came from one doesn't know.

"It might be Cosmo Lang. It might be anyone. I cannot prove or disprove."

A point that worried the Bishop and the other two clergymen was that the discarnate Lang was less lucid and his arguments less clear cut than they expected. Lang when alive was a brilliant speaker.

Pearce-Higgins finds this no difficulty.

"It is impossible," he says, "to expect the voice of a discarnate person to be exactly the same as the living voice when you consider the difficulties with which it is produced.

"It seems the intelligence gets clouded in the descent from their high levels to our low ones.

"It is difficult for them to get through to us at all. They cannot express themselves as clearly as they can in their normal state—or even as well as they did on earth.

"They do sometimes, therefore, seem to function on a lower level than they did when they were alive on earth."

Is it possible to get any nearer to the truth than that?

No-one can say for certain.

* * *

Books connected to or referenced in the Chapters.

Chapter One:

An Extraordinary Journey – The Memoirs of a Physical Medium by Stewart Alexander. (ISBN 9781786771377)

Chapter Two:

Alec Harris – The full story of his remarkable physical mediumship by Louie Harris. (ISBN 9780955705045)

An Extraordinary Journey – The Memoirs of a Physical Medium by Stewart Alexander. (ISBN 9781786771377)

Touching the Next Horizon by Katie Halliwell (ISBN 9781908421470)

What is the Next Horizon? by Katie Halliwell. (ISBN 9781908421623)

Life After Death – Living Proof by Tom Harrison. (ISBN 9780955705014)

Red Cloud's Inner Teachings Volume I & II by Brandon J. Kim. (ISBN 9798454224332)

Mediumship: Our Heritage by Kate Maesen; Rev. John C. Lilek and Rev. Dr. James Garfield Tingley D.D. (ISBN 9781838359454)

Experiences of Physical Phenomena in the 21st Century by Ann E. Harrison (ISBN 9781908421609)

Great Moments of Modern Mediumship - Volumes 1 & 2 by Maxine Meilleur (Vol 1 ISBN 9781908421104) / Vol2 (ISBN 9781908421180)

Chapter Three:

Voices in the Dark by Leslie Flint (In print form) from https://www.leslieflint.com/voices-in-the-dark.

An excellent book on the voices that came through Leslie Flint is **'Life After Death'** by Neville Randall (1975) and is available as an ebook (available from Nook, Apple Books, Kobo, Everand and many other ebook retailers & online libraries) – or in print (second hand).

An Extraordinary Journey – The Memoirs of a Physical Medium by Stewart Alexander (ISBN 9781786771377)

On the Edge of the Etheric by Arthur Findlay (ISBN 9781585093403),

Chapter Four:

Of Love between Two Worlds by Georgina & Robert Brake. (ISBN 9781908421012) (only available from www.snpp.com)

What is the Next Horizon? by Katie Halliwell. (ISBN 9781908421623)

Chapter Five:

Alec Harris – The full story of his remarkable physical mediumship by Louie Harris. (ISBN 9780955705045)

What is the Next Horizon? by Katie Halliwell. (ISBN 9781908421623)

www.ingramcontent.com/pod-product-compliance
Lightning Source LLC
Chambersburg PA
CBHW071221070526
44584CB00019B/3112